Art Director	Charles Matheson
Art Editor	Ben White
Editor	James McCarter
Illustrators	Denis Bishop
	Chris Forsey
	Hayward Art Group
	Jim Robins

Designed and produced by
Aladdin Books Ltd
70 Old Compton Street
London W1

*First published in the
United States in 1983 by*
Franklin Watts
387 Park Avenue South
New York, NY 10016

ISBN 531–04652-4

Library of Congress
Catalog Card No: 83-50114

Printed in Belgium

Franklin Watts Science World

Physics

Nigel Henbest and Heather Couper

Series Editor: Lionel Bender

FRANKLIN WATTS
New York · London · Toronto · Sydney

Introduction

Physics is the science of matter and energy. It studies how matter behaves under different conditions, and looks at how matter and energy interact. Everything in the Universe consists of matter, and every event, from a star exploding to you kicking a football, requires energy to make it happen, so physics covers a huge range of subjects.

We begin by looking at forces and motion, and discover that just three basic laws describe the relationship between the two. One branch of the study of forces – statics – leads to an explanation of how pulleys and levers can be used to increase the forces we apply.

The next chapter concerns the nature of matter itself. What is the fundamental difference between solids, liquids and gases? The answer lies in the way that atoms – the incredibly small building blocks of matter – join together to form molecules, and in the way that these molecules themselves link up. The movement of these molecules forms the basis for understanding the next two subjects dealt with – heat and sound. The book then moves on to the study of light. We look in detail at how mirrors and lenses work, and at what causes the different colors we see in the rainbow.

Finally, we see how physics explains the two closely related subjects of electricity and magnetism in terms of the tiny electrons found within every atom. Only by understanding what causes electricity, and how it behaves, have we been able to develop the technology of such things as television, telephones, and computers, that now surround us in everyday life.

Because physics covers so many subjects it is divided into several sections. *Dynamics* and *Statics* deals with the way that forces act on objects, whether the object is a speeding car or a balanced see-saw. And the study of *Sound* provides explanations that apply equally to the roar of a jetliner and the quietest music. The fact that *Light* travels in waves leads to an explanation of properties such as color and reflection. And by looking into the atom, physicists have found that *Electricity* and *Magnetism* are closely related – a relationship demonstrated by, for instance, electric motors.

Balancing forces

Sound

Contents

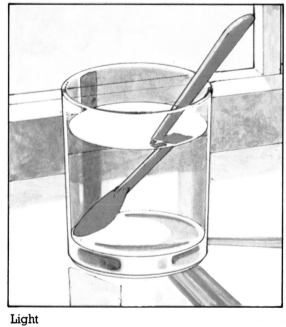

Light

Electricity and magnetism

Forces and Motion

All of our activities, from picking up this book to demolishing a skyscraper, depend upon using forces. Forces cause objects to move, and the study of forces is called "dynamics." In dynamics, the connection between force and movement is summed up in three laws of motion.

The first law states that an object at rest, or one which is moving in a straight line at a steady speed, will remain in that state unless a force acts upon it. In everyday life we cannot escape from forces completely. The force of Earth's gravity is always there, pulling everything downward. And the truck shown here leaving the demolition site also has the forces of wind resistance and friction (the effect of the ground "dragging" against its wheels), acting to slow it down.

Law two says that when a force *does* act upon an object, it changes the object's speed or direction of travel to a degree which depends on the strength of the force and the mass ("weight") of the object. The more force the worker uses to swing his hammer, the faster it will go, but the heavier the hammer is, the harder it is to swing.

The third law states that whenever a force is applied, then there is always an equal force acting in the opposite direction. When we push against a desk, for example, we feel a force pushing us backward, and when we walk, we push back on the ground, and the equal and opposite force pushes us forward.

▷ Whenever we need movement, we must use a force to produce it. The powerful force of the heavy ball crashing against the wall causes the bricks to move, cracking their cement bonding. They then fall to the ground under the force of the Earth's gravity.

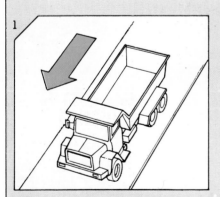

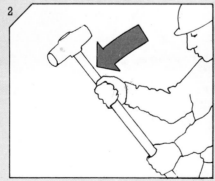

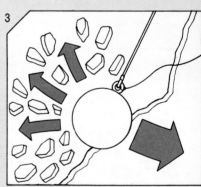

The three laws of motion
The force of gravity causes this truck to roll downhill. If there were no forces acting on it, then "law one" says that it would remain stationary.

The worker uses the force of his muscles and the force of gravity to swing his hammer downward. The heavier the hammer, the more force it will transfer on impact.

Every action has an equal and opposite reaction. The heavy ball transfers enough force on impact to break the wall, but the wall's opposite reaction stops its swing.

Gravity

Astronaut on the Moon

The force of Earth's gravity pulls everything downward giving us weight. Weight is simply gravity's pull. Physicists call the amount of matter an object has its *mass*. An astronaut has the same *mass* on the Moon as he does on Earth, but he weighs only a sixth as much. This is because the Moon is smaller than the Earth, and therefore has less mass, and so exerts a weaker gravitational force on the astronaut. All objects exert gravitational force, and the more massive an object is, the greater is its gravity.

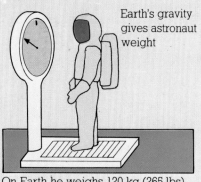

Earth's gravity gives astronaut weight

On Earth he weighs 120 kg (265 lbs)

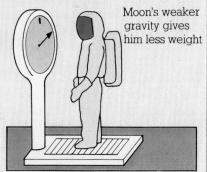

Moon's weaker gravity gives him less weight

On the Moon he weighs 20 kg (44 lbs)

Circular Motion

Objects which travel in a circle, such as this model plane, are a special case of objects moving under a force. The force acting on them is directed toward the center of the circle. You can feel this if you whirl a ball around on a string. Instead of changing the ball's speed, this force – called centripetal force – is continually changing the ball's direction of travel. Once the centripetal force is removed – by letting go of the string – the ball ceases to change its direction of travel, and flies off in a straight line, as the first law of motion now applies.

Flying a model aircraft

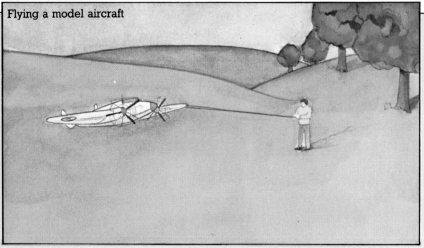

Red arrows represent force
Blue arrows represent motion

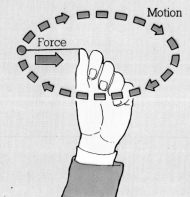

Motion

Force

Motion

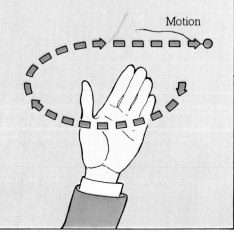

Momentum

The railway wagon on the left speeds down the slope toward the stationary wagon. Both have the same mass, and when they collide, they link up and travel forward at half the speed of the first wagon. This illustrates a basic principle of physics which states that *momentum* remains constant. Momentum is measured by multiplying the mass of an object by its speed. Because the coupled wagons have double the mass of the single wagon, they must travel at half the speed of the first wagon.

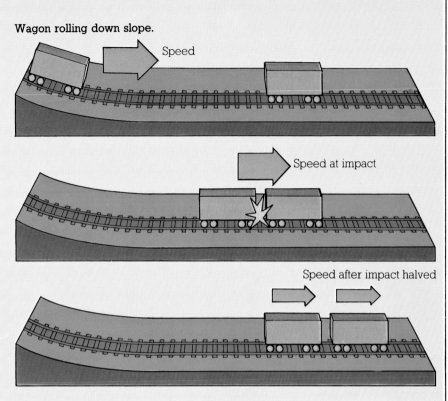

Wagon rolling down slope.

Speed

Speed at impact

Speed after impact halved

Energy

An archer

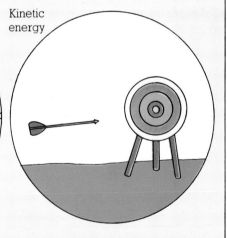

Potential energy

Kinetic energy

Energy is the ability to move force from one point to another, but an object does not have to move to have energy. It can have the potential to transmit force because of its position. Physicists call this energy *potential* energy. An arrow in a drawn-back bow has potential energy. When the bowstring is released this potential energy is changed into the energy of movement – *kinetic* energy. When the arrow hits the target, kinetic energy changes into *heat* energy, caused by friction on the arrow head as it pierces the wood. Energy changes its form, but it is never lost or destroyed.

Balancing Forces

The high wire act is usually the climax of the circus show. The audience holds its breath as the spotlight picks out the tightrope walker high up above the circus ring.

There are two main forces acting on the tightrope walker. Gravity pulls his body and the balancing pole downward, and the wire pushes upward to support this combined weight. Because there are no forces "left over," there is nothing to cause any movement. The balancing of a number of different forces to leave a body stationary is called "statics."

Although gravity pulls on all parts of our body, we can think of our weight being concentrated in the center of our body. This point is called the "center of gravity," and the weights on either side of it are equal. The tightrope walker uses his pole to make sure that his center of gravity is always directly above the rope. If he leans slightly to one side, then his center of gravity shifts, and he needs to place his pole to the opposite side, so that the weight of the pole balances his weight around their joint center of gravity.

▷ A tightrope walker uses the principles of statics – the cancelling out of forces and turning moments – to keep himself balanced on the high wire. The same principles are used by the circus's other balancing acts, such as the bareback riders and the acrobats in the human pyramid.

When forces act at a distance from the center of gravity they have a tipping effect, like pulling down one side of a see-saw. This tipping effect is called the "turning moment" of the force, and in statics, the turning moments of all the forces acting on an object must cancel each other out for that object to remain balanced.

Statics is a very important subject for architects and engineers. If the forces and turning moments acting on, for example, a building or a bridge, were not lined up, then they would eventually cause the structure to crack and fall. Similarly, the turning moments acting on engine parts and on machines such as cranes must be balanced to prevent their failure.

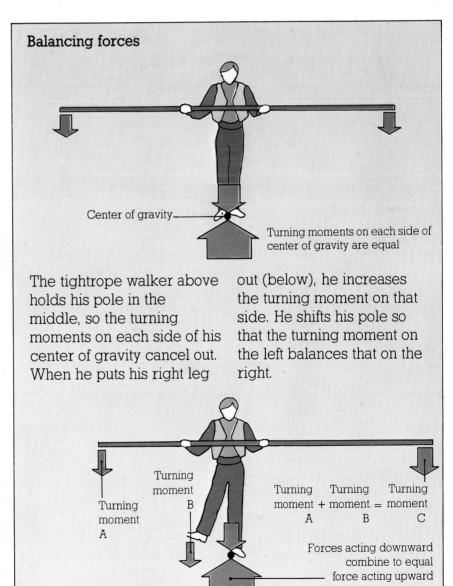

Balancing forces

Center of gravity

Turning moments on each side of center of gravity are equal

The tightrope walker above holds his pole in the middle, so the turning moments on each side of his center of gravity cancel out. When he puts his right leg out (below), he increases the turning moment on that side. He shifts his pole so that the turning moment on the left balances that on the right.

Turning moment A

Turning moment B

Turning moment A + Turning moment B = Turning moment C

Forces acting downward combine to equal force acting upward

Turning Moments

A see-saw balances the turning moments of the weights of the two children. A lightweight child can balance a heavy child only if they both sit in the correct place to create equal turning moments about the see-saw's fulcrum. The turning moment is worked out by multiplying the weight of a child by its distance from the fulcrum. If the girl weighs only half as much as the boy, then she must sit twice as far from the fulcrum for the turning moments to be equal and cancel each other out.

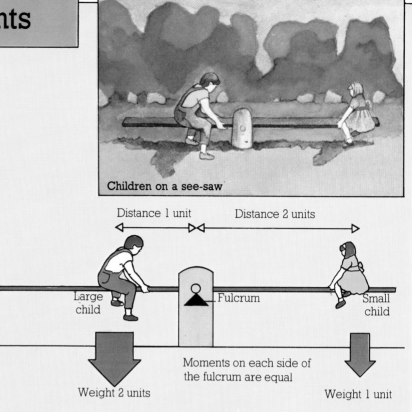

Children on a see-saw

Distance 1 unit — Distance 2 units

Large child

Fulcrum

Small child

Moments on each side of the fulcrum are equal

Weight 2 units

Weight 1 unit

Resultant Force

What happens when two forces act on an object in different directions? When a boat is rowed across a river, for example, the force of the oars pushes it forward, while the force of the river's current sweeps the boat downstream. How can we work out how the boat will travel under these two forces? If we represent each force by a line, drawn in the direction that the force is acting, and to a length proportional to the strength of each force, then we can construct a "triangle of forces." The third side of the triangle shows how the forces combine to produce a "resultant force." This resultant force carries the boat well downstream.

Rowing across a river in a strong current

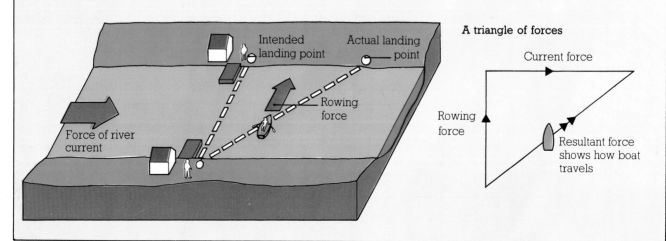

Intended landing point

Actual landing point

Rowing force

Force of river current

A triangle of forces

Current force

Rowing force

Resultant force shows how boat travels

Multiplying Forces

Levers

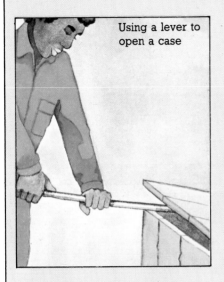

Using a lever to open a case

When we use a lever, we are using turning moments to increase the force we can exert. Opening a packing case, for example, we exert force on the longer arm of the lever. Because the turning moments on either side of the fulcrum (the edge of the case) must be equal, the force exerted by the shorter arm of the lever on the case's lid must be greater.

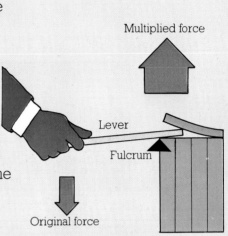

Multiplied force

Lever

Fulcrum

Original force

Pulleys

Using pulleys to lift a heavy weight

One mechanic can lift a heavy car engine using pulleys. Two pulleys are firmly fixed to a beam. The mechanic pulls a rope which goes around each pulley in turn. All four strands of rope carry the force that the mechanic exerts, so the total force lifting the engine is, in this case, four times the mechanic's pull. Some force is lost due to friction between the rope and the pulley.

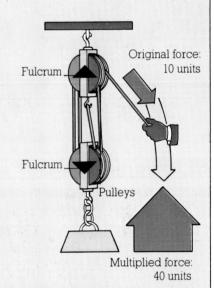

Fulcrum

Original force: 10 units

Fulcrum

Pulleys

Multiplied force: 40 units

Gears

Using gears to transmit force

Different-sized wheels, or gears, connected together can also increase or decrease forces. In the arrangement here, the large gear wheel has four times the number of teeth or cogs as the smaller one. Each time the large gear turns once, the smaller gear, turning the rear wheel, turns four times. The rear wheel receives only one-quarter the force, but turns four times as fast as the pedals.

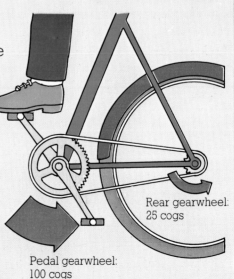

Rear gearwheel: 25 cogs

Pedal gearwheel: 100 cogs

Solids, Liquids and Gases

In an operating theater, the oxygen that the patient needs to breathe, perhaps for a total of two or three hours, can be stored in a small metal cylinder. This is because oxygen is a gas, and gases can easily be compressed in volume. Liquids, on the other hand, resist compression. Liquids flow freely, and this fact allows the patient's blood to circulate through his body, and to pass through monitoring equipment. Both gases and liquids need to be held in a solid container – gases because they will expand to fill any available volume, and liquids because they have no fixed shape of their own. Solids are rigid, and keep the shape which they have.

Solid, liquid and gas are known as the three states of matter, and each has its own particular property. The reason for these differences lies in the fundamental building blocks of matter itself – atoms. Atoms are particles so tiny that they cannot be seen, even using the most powerful microscope. Atoms join together to form molecules, and these molecules in turn join up in a way which determines the state that a substance has.

In solids, the bonds between molecules are strong and rigid, holding each molecule in a fixed position. In liquids, the molecules are packed close together, but the bonds between them are very weak, so while liquids are hard to compress, they are still able to flow freely. Gases expand freely and are easy to compress because the molecules are separate and have no bonds between them.

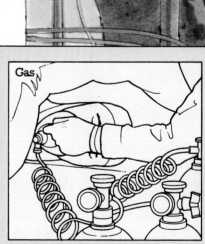

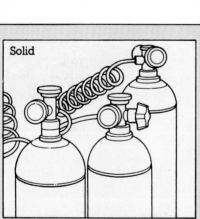

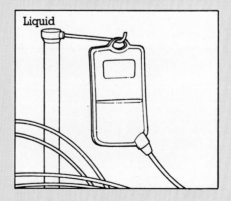

The three states of matter

Solids, once they have been made into a particular shape, will keep that shape because of the strong bonds linking their molecules.

Liquids must be held in containers, as their molecular bonds are weak, so that liquids take the shape of the container holding them.

Gases expand to fill all available space. A mixture of nitric oxide gas (an anaesthetic), and oxygen is supplied to the patient.

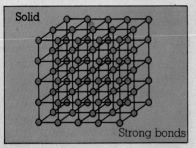

Solid

Strong bonds

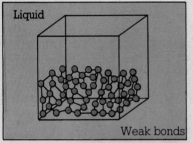

Liquid

Weak bonds

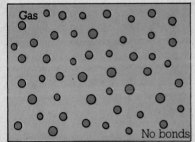

Gas

No bonds

Properties of each state
The key to the different
characteristics of the three
states of matter lies in the
bonds between their
molecules. Often, in solids,
these bonds are arranged
in a regular way, and this
gives them a "crystalline"
structure. Common salt is
a good example: under a
magnifying glass you can
see that it has a regular,
square, crystal structure.
Liquids have far weaker
bonds, and gases have
none at all.

Density

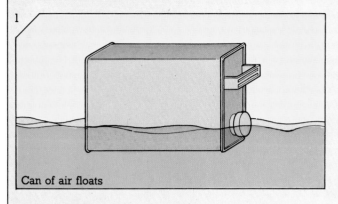

1

Can of air floats

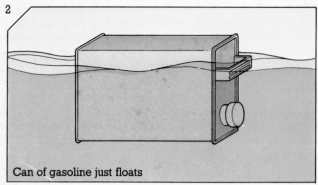

2

Can of gasoline just floats

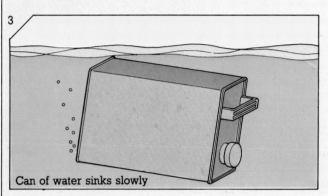

3

Can of water sinks slowly

4

Solid lump of metal sinks fast

A substance's density is a measure of the weight of material within a certain volume. This indicates how tightly "packed" the molecules of that substance are. A can containing air – a gas – will float in water because its density is less than that of water (1). Filled with gasoline, the can *just* floats, showing that gasoline is less dense than water (2). Fill the can with water and it sinks, because the density of the can plus water is greater than the density of water itself (3). A lump of metal plummets to the bottom (4). A giant oil tanker will float at different levels, depending on the weight and density of its load.

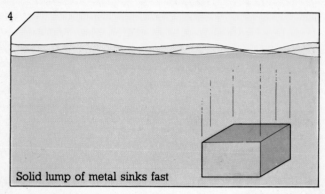

Lightly laden

Heavily laden

Tankers with different weight loads

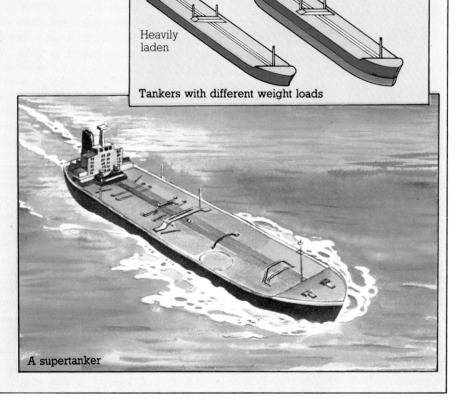

A supertanker

Compression

What happens when gases are compressed? If you take a bicycle pump and place your finger firmly over the end, you can compress the air inside to an ever-smaller volume. As the molecules of the gas become more and more tightly packed, it becomes harder and harder to push the plunger in further, as the pressure of the gas increases. In fact, if enough force was applied, the molecules would be so tightly packed together that the gas would become a liquid. If you tried to do the same experiment with the

Squeezing a gas

pump full of water, you would find that you would be unable to push the plunger in at all. This is because the molecules of a liquid are so tightly packed that they offer very great resistance to forces of compression.

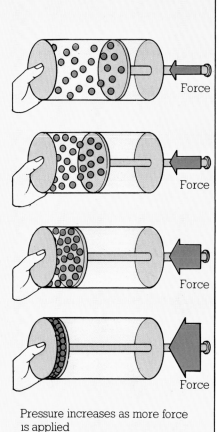

Force

Force

Force

Force

Pressure increases as more force is applied

Elasticity

When the force stretching an elastic band is removed, the band returns to its normal size. Even metals

Weighing a fish

have this property of elasticity, particularly when they are in the shape of a spring. What happens is that the molecular bonds themselves stretch when a force is applied, and when the force is removed the bonds cause the molecules to take up their normal position. This elastic property can be used to weigh things, because the spring stretches by an amount that is proportional to the weight, or force, pulling on it: a fish that is twice as heavy as another will stretch the spring twice as much.

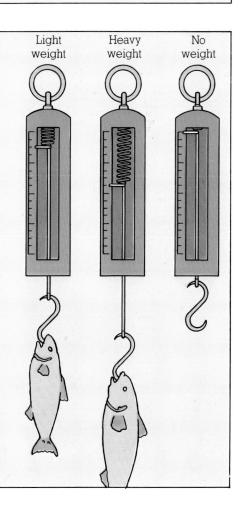

Light weight   Heavy weight   No weight

Heat Energy

The highest mountain peaks are covered with snow all year round, and mountaineers need protective clothing to keep out the cold. Hot soup at base camp helps them keep their spirits up. To make the soup, a few handfuls of snow can be melted in their saucepan and heated up.

Heat is a form of energy. When the snow is heated, it is being given extra energy, and this energy is in the form of molecular movement. The water molecules in snow are held in fixed bonds, and when heat is added these molecules vibrate more and more strongly until the bonds holding them together break, and solid snow becomes liquid water. As the heating continues, the free molecules of liquid water move about with ever-increasing speed. Eventually they move so fast that they escape from their partners altogether, and the liquid becomes a gas: water changes to steam.

When substances are cooled, their molecules slow down. At an extremely low temperature of approximately −273°C (−460°F) the molecules almost stop moving completely, and they have virtually no heat energy. It is impossible to make anything colder than this, so this temperature is called Absolute Zero.

Heat energy is put to work in many aspects of the modern world. In power stations, for example, the heat energy created by burning fuel is used to produce steam. The energy of the fast-moving molecules in the steam is used to power the generators that produce electricity. And all of our forms of transport – cars, trucks, locomotives, ships and jetliners – have engines that convert heat energy to the energy of motion.

▷ Heat energy causes a substance to change its state. The molecular bonds of ice are strong enough to support the weight of the mountaineers. At higher temperatures ice becomes an invisible gas – steam. The clouds of "steam" rising from the saucepan are tiny droplets of water, formed as the steam cools down.

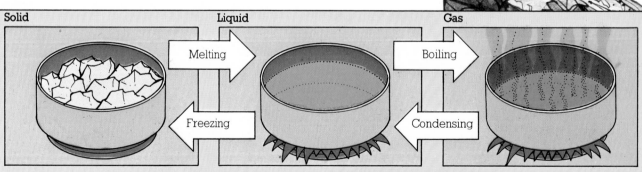

Solid	Liquid	Gas
Melting →	Boiling →	
← Freezing	← Condensing	

The effect of heat on matter

Heat causes the water molecules in ice to break their bonds, and the ice becomes water. The water molecules move faster as more heat is applied. Eventually they fly about freely as a gas: steam. The steam cools to water vapor, and if cooling is continued the process is reversed and the water becomes ice.

Boiling spaghetti

Convection

Heat travels in liquids and gases by "convection." As the cooker heats the pan the water at the bottom becomes hotter. Hot water has a lower density than cold because its molecules are moving faster. As a result, the hot water rises and forces the cooler water down. This movement is known as a "convection current," and can be seen to twist the strands of spaghetti in the pan.

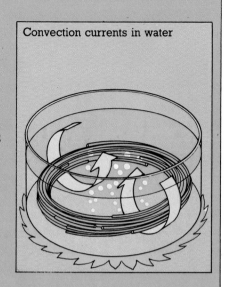
Convection currents in water

A coal fire

Conduction

The fire heating one end of a poker causes the molecules there to vibrate more vigorously. These molecules jostle their neighbors further along the poker. This increases their vibration, so passing heat along. Most metals conduct heat well, but substances such as wood or asbestos do not, so a wooden handle can protect our hands from the heat conducted along the poker.

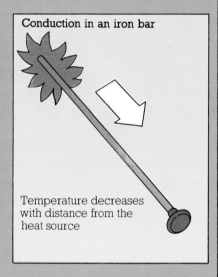
Conduction in an iron bar

Temperature decreases with distance from the heat source

The Sun

Radiation

Convection and conduction cannot carry heat through a vacuum where there are no molecules to vibrate. But heat from the Sun reaches us after crossing the vacuum of space. In this case, heat travels in the form of radiation. Heat radiation is very similar to light, but it is invisible. It has a wavelength slightly longer than that of red light, so scientists call heat radiation *infrared* radiation. Infrared warms us when we sunbathe.

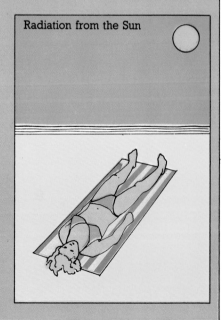
Radiation from the Sun

Heat at Work

A steam locomotive

One of the first machines to put heat energy to work was the steam engine, still in use in some locomotives. The engine burns coal in its firebox to create the heat source. The flames heat the water in the boiler to turn it to steam. As a gas, steam expands to take up more space than water. When confined in a cylinder, the force of the gas molecules produces a pressure which pushes a sliding piston in the cylinder. The piston pushes a drive shaft which turns the locomotive's driving wheels, so propelling the train.

Steam

Water

Heat source

Force of steam under pressure

Motion

Drive shaft

Piston inside cylinder

Steam out

Wheel

Expansion

Heat causes substances to expand because of their increased molecular movement. This effect is used in a thermometer to measure temperature. The thermometer contains a liquid (usually mercury or alcohol). As the liquid is heated by its surroundings, it expands up the graded tube to a level that indicates the temperature. The choice of a temperature scale is a matter of convenience. Most countries use the Celsius scale (also called Centigrade), in which the melting point of ice is

Thermometer in a greenhouse

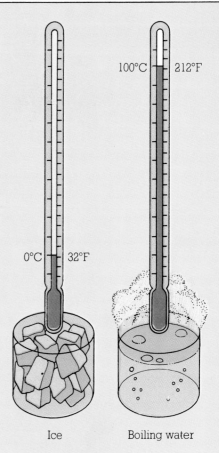

100°C   212°F

0°C   32°F

zero degrees, and the boiling point of water 100 degrees. The scale is then divided equally between these two points. Some countries use the Fahrenheit scale. Ice melts at 32 degrees Fahrenheit and water boils at 212 degrees.

Ice

Boiling water

Sound

At the climax of a great symphony, the orchestra fills a concert hall with a thrilling crescendo of sound. But some of the quietest passages may be so soft that you can hardly hear the sound of an instrument as it is played. But sound doesn't differ just in volume. It also varies in pitch. The low-pitched notes of a double bass can almost make the floor vibrate, while some of the notes of the flute or violin are almost piercingly high.

All sounds are caused by movement, whether they sound as beautiful as the violin or as painful as a large jet roaring to takeoff. The movement at the source of the sound sets up a vibration in the molecules of the air. These molecules jostle neighboring molecules, and so the vibration is carried to our ears. Inside our ears, the air vibrates against our eardrums, and we hear the sound. In space, where there is no air, sound cannot travel.

The difference between sounds is a result of the difference in the movements that cause them. Quiet sounds are the result of a gentle vibration that causes only a small disturbance in the air molecules. Loud sounds are created by violent disturbances that can sometimes be powerful enough to damage our ears.

▽ A modern symphony orchestra uses a wide range of different instruments. Guided by the conductor, the musicians create every combination of pitch and loudness to convey the composer's music to the best effect. But each note is simply the result of vibrations in the air.

The difference in pitch between two sounds is the result of the *rate* at which the air vibrates, which in turn depends on the rate of vibration of the sound source. The quicker the rate of vibration, the higher the pitch of the note produced. On stringed instruments, the pitch is changed by changing the length of the string being plucked or struck. In wind instruments, different notes are produced by covering or uncovering holes in the tube in which the air is made to vibrate – the stem of an oboe, for example, or the sleeve of a trombone.

The rhythmical vibration of the air molecules as the sound is transmitted away from its source is called a sound wave. Sound waves travel through air in almost the same way as waves travel in water. They have been measured to travel at a speed of 1,226 km/h (750 miles/h). This speed is the same for every sound, whether it is loud or soft, high-pitched or low-pitched. When an aircraft travels faster than this a "sonic boom" is heard, caused by the sound waves crowding so close together that they create a shock wave, which we hear as the "boom." Sonic booms can be powerful enough to crack the glass in greenhouses underneath the aircraft's path.

What is sound?

When the kettledrum is struck, its skin vibrates. As the skin moves upward, the air molecules above it are compressed, while on its downward movement they are drawn apart, creating a *rarefaction*. These bands of compression and rarefaction are the peaks and troughs of the sound wave.

Rarefaction

Compression

Compression

Sound as a wave-form

Rarefaction

Direction of wave →

Wave-form

Sound waves spread out like ripples on a pond, becoming weaker the further they travel. By studying graphs of sound waves we can see how they are made up. By looking at the amplitudes, or wave-peaks, of a soft sound (1) and a loud sound (2), we can see that the soft sound makes only slight compressions in the air, while the loud sound compresses the air more strongly. The distance between two wave-peaks is called the *wavelength*. Musical notes with a higher pitch (3) have shorter wavelengths than bass notes, since the air molecules are compressed more often. The number of compressions a wave makes a second is its *frequency*.

A ripple in a pond

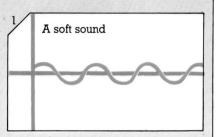

1 A soft sound

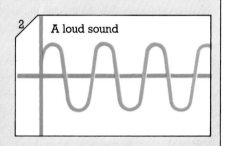

2 A loud sound

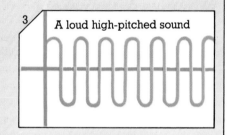

3 A loud high-pitched sound

Echoes

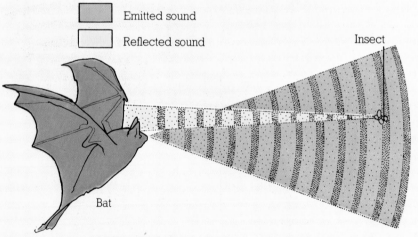

A bat hunting for food

Emitted sound

Reflected sound

Insect

Bat

When a sound wave hits a solid object, it "bounces" back in an echo. You can hear an echo if you clap your hands when standing at a distance from the base of a cliff. If you measure your distance from the cliff, you can work out how fast sound waves travel, by doubling the distance (the sound reaches the cliff and then travels back to you) and dividing it by the time taken. Bats use sound echoes to enable them to fly in the dark and seek out their prey. Bats "sing" very high-pitched notes (often so high that people cannot hear them) at a rate of about ten pulses a second. Their very sensitive ears pick up the echoes from any obstacles in their flight path, or from prey, such as a tiny fly. The direction of the echo tells the bat the direction in which the object lies, and the time delay between echoes indicates its distance.

Making Music

A harp – a stringed instrument

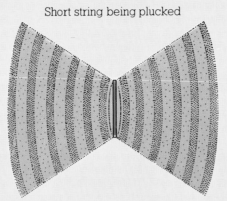
Short string being plucked

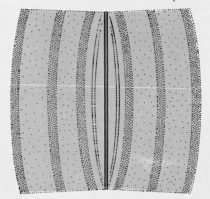
Long string being plucked

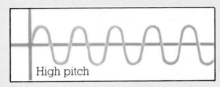
High pitch

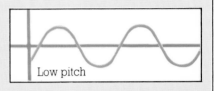
Low pitch

The strings of different lengths on a harp produce notes of different pitch. A short string vibrates very quickly when plucked, creating a sound wave with a short wavelength and, therefore, high pitch. Longer strings vibrate more slowly, creating low-pitched sounds.

An organ – a wind instrument

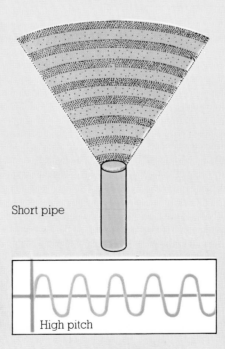
Short pipe
High pitch

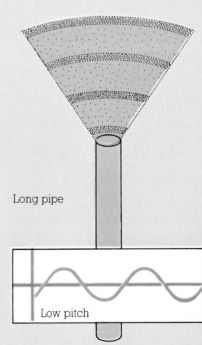
Long pipe
Low pitch

In wind instruments, such as the organ, notes are created by air vibrating in a pipe or tube. Notes of different pitch are created by varying the length of the pipe. The air in the shortest pipes vibrates most rapidly, giving a high-pitched note. Long pipes create the low-pitched notes.

Light

Sunlight reflected off the sea can be dazzling on a bright day, and the Sun's heat can be fierce enough to damage our skin. As we have seen, heat from the Sun reaches us by radiation. Light is just another form of radiation given off by the Sun, but one which, unlike heat, can be detected by our eyes.

Both light and radiant heat travel as waves. The only difference between the two is in their wavelength, just as the only difference between two sounds of different pitch is in their wavelength. Radiant heat has a longer wavelength than visible light. Ultraviolet radiation, the radiation that causes tanning, has a shorter wavelength than light. In fact, the Sun gives off a huge range of radiations of different wavelengths, and physicists call this the "electromagnetic spectrum."

All the waves in the electromagnetic spectrum travel at the same speed as they cross the vacuum of space – an astonishing 300,000 km/sec (186,000 miles/sec). But when they encounter substances such as water or air, this speed is decreased, as the atoms and molecules of that substance absorb some of their energy. Some substances absorb the energy of light completely – light cannot pass through them and they cast a shadow.

Although light can pass through substances such as air, water, and glass, it can be seen to be affected by them. The girl's fishing net appears to be bent as it enters the water, and the small boy can see a reflection of himself as he leans over the edge of the pool.

▷ On a bright summer day by the sea, so much of the Sun's light reaches us that you can see things that you might not have noticed before. The shadows seem that much more definite. The reflections are extra bright, and the bottom of a pool seems closer than it really is.

Properties of light

Shadows

Light cannot pass through our bodies, and so we cast a shadow. This shows that light cannot bend around us, but travels in straight lines.

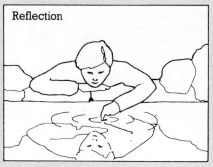

Reflection

Light does penetrate through water to an extent, but some is also reflected off the surface, so that the pool acts as a mirror.

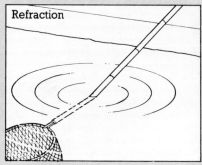

Refraction

Light waves entering water are slowed down, so that they deceive the eye. This makes the rod look bent and the floor of the pool seem closer.

The first effect, the bending of the rod, is a phenomenon called *refraction*, and is caused by the different optical densities of air and water. Water is denser than air, so it slows the light waves down, causing the optical illusion. Reflection is the result of light waves "bouncing" back off an object. Light waves from the Sun reflect off the boy's face onto the surface of the water, which in turn reflects the light back into his eyes.

Remember, *never* look at the Sun directly, even through smoked glass, sun glasses, or fogged film. The Sun's radiation is so powerful that your eyesight could be seriously, and permanently, damaged.

Reflection

Highly polished surfaces – a silver plate, for example – reflect the light falling on them without any distortion. They act as mirrors, and most mirrors are made of highly polished glass with a silvered backing. Light is reflected off a flat mirror at exactly the same angle as it hits it, just as when a ball is thrown at a wall, it bounces off at the same angle with which it struck. In other words, the angle of incidence – angle A – is equal to the angle of reflection – angle B. One consequence of this is that when you look in the mirror everything appears to be reversed left to right. The girl in the picture is holding her hairbrush in her right hand, but the mirror shows an image of her holding the brush in her left hand. Every other feature is "inverted" in the same way.

Normal

Angle A | Angle B

Incident ray

Reflected ray

Mirror

Angle A and angle B are equal

Refraction

Refraction is the bending of light when it passes from one medium to another. When the light hits the glass block, some of it is reflected. The rest is bent downward. When it leaves the block at the bottom surface, refraction causes the light to be bent back again by the same angle. A magnifying glass is curved, and this causes the light to be bent inward at both surfaces. Our eyes see this light as if it had not been bent, and receive the image of the much larger "virtual" fly rather than the real one.

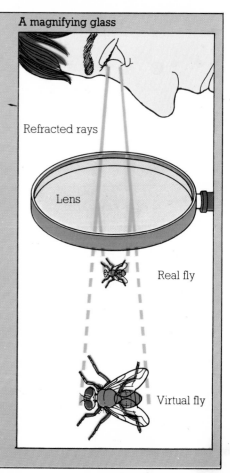

Refracted rays

Lens

Real fly

Virtual fly

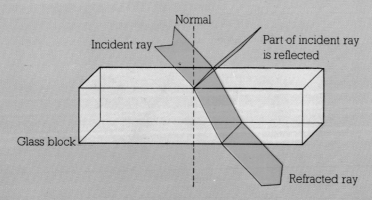

Normal

Incident ray

Part of incident ray is reflected

Glass block

Refracted ray

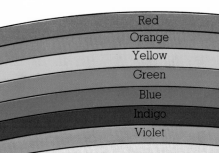

Red
Orange
Yellow
Green
Blue
Indigo
Violet

A rainbow

The color wheel

The Spectrum

A rainbow is caused by the refraction of sunlight passing through water droplets in the atmosphere after a rainstorm. Light is a radiation composed of different wavelengths. Short wavelength light, which we see as violet, is refracted (bent) the most, while long wavelength light (red) is bent least. The result is that light is spread out into the different colors, and wavelengths, that we see in the rainbow.

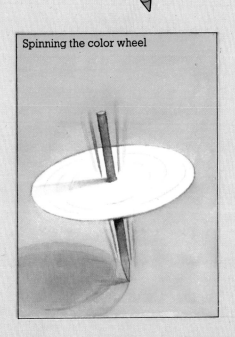

Spinning the color wheel

The opposite effect can be created by spinning a disk painted with rainbow colors. As the different colors merge, the disk turns an off-white color. A sheet of paper is white because it reflects all the wavelengths of light back into our eyes. Coal is black because all the wavelengths are absorbed – black is simply an absence of light. Grass is green because it reflects light of green wavelength and absorbs other wavelengths.

Splitting light

An artificial rainbow – a spectrum – can be produced by passing sunlight through a narrow slit and into a triangular glass block called a prism. This splits the light into its seven main colors, as the light of different wavelengths is refracted to a different degree.

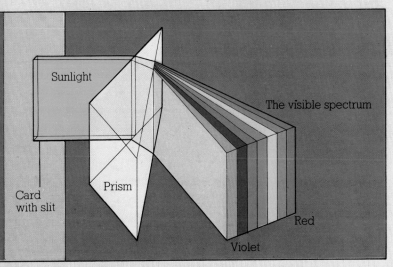

Sunlight

The visible spectrum

Card with slit

Prism

Violet

Red

Electricity

The sudden violence of a lightning flash can be frightening, but lightning is no more than a dramatic display of electricity in action.

Lightning is caused by a stream of tiny particles called electrons. Every atom has a cloud of electrons circling its central core, or nucleus. Electrons have a property called electric charge, as does the atom's nucleus. But these two charges are different. The electron's charge is negative, while that of the nucleus is positive. Negative and positive charges attract one another. Electricity is caused when electrons escape from their atom and seek to join up with particles having a positive charge.

In a thunderstorm, some electrons are removed from their atoms by the friction of dust or ice particles rubbing together. An area of negative electrons gradually builds up. In comparison to this area the Earth has a positive charge. When the build-up of charge becomes strong enough, the electrons stream to the Earth in the lightning flash.

Electricity has great energy, and, fortunately, we can control this energy when the electrons flow along a metal wire. Today's world depends on electrical energy. We use it to light our homes and streets, to power industrial machines and our telephone and television networks, and in a huge range of other ways, all of them based on controlling the power of tiny electrons.

▽ Most tall buildings are protected from lightning by having metal lightning conductors. The electrons can travel more easily through metal than through the building, and so they take this path to Earth.

Removing electrons

The heavy nucleus of an atom contains charged particles called protons. These have a charge that is equal in strength, but opposite in charge to electrons. One electron will just neutralize or balance the charge of a proton. Thus, a proton-electron pair is neutral. An atom has the same number of positively charged protons as it has electrons, so the charges cancel out. But when an electron is taken away, the atom is left with an unpaired proton, giving it a positive charge. When you comb your hair, electrons are rubbed off onto the comb, giving it a negative charge. Your hair is left with a positive charge. Unlike charges attract, so your hair rises up toward the comb. When the two touch, their charges cancel out.

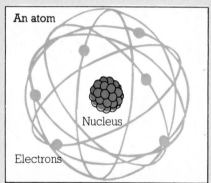

An atom

Nucleus

Electrons

Electrons lost from hair to comb

Lightning
Negatively-charged electrons build up at the base of a storm cloud. Eventually, the build-up becomes so intense that the electrons stream to the positively-charged Earth in a huge lightning bolt.

Cloud base

Negative charge

Positive charge

Earth

The Flow of Electrons

A conductor is a material that lets electrons move within it. Metals are the best conductors. Electrons from the metal atoms drift from the negative end of the wire to the positive end, creating the electric current. The direction of current is shown as opposite to the electron flow, a custom dating from before electrons were known. These are known as conventional current and electron current.

An electric circuit

An electric current will only flow if both ends of the conductor are connected to form a circuit. It also needs a force to drive it round this circuit. This is the *electron-moving force* (EMF), and is measured in units called *volts*. The amount of energy the current carries through the circuit depends on the strength of the electron-moving force driving it round.

Using a torch

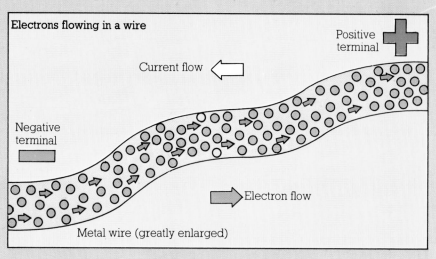

Electrons flowing in a wire

Positive terminal

Current flow

Negative terminal

Electron flow

Metal wire (greatly enlarged)

Note: although electrons actually flow from (−) to (+) terminals, "conventional" current is said to flow in the opposite direction.

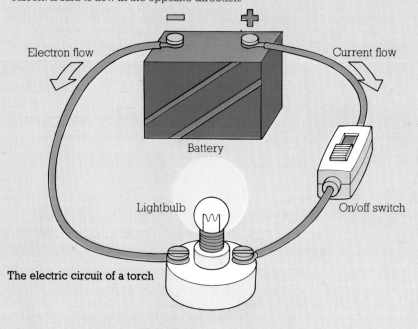

Electron flow

Current flow

Battery

Lightbulb

On/off switch

The electric circuit of a torch

Physicists measure current in units called *amperes*, often shortened to just *amps*. These two units – volts and amps – multiplied together determine the power that the electric circuit can produce. Electrical power is measured in *watts* – you may have noticed that lightbulbs are often marked as being 40, 60 or 100 watts. This is a measure of the electric power the bulbs use, and, partly, the amount of light they emit. In the circuit above, the electron-moving force is supplied by a battery, and the circuit supplies power to a small lightbulb. The on/off switch simply makes or breaks the circuit as a convenient way to control the electric current. You can find a similar circuit in an ordinary pocket flashlight.

Resistance

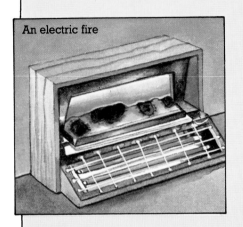
An electric fire

Reflecting panel

High resistance wire produces heat
energy from electric current

When electrons travel in a conductor, they experience a resistance to their motion. This comes from the atoms in it. Some conductors offer more resistance than others. Iron, for example, offers seven times the resistance of copper. As the electrons force their way through the circuit, they jostle the atoms of the wire, causing them to vibrate. Vibrating atoms and molecules give out their energy as heat. In an electric fire a high resistance wire heats up, and this heat is directed outward by a reflecting panel. The same principle is used in electric stoves.

Directing Electrons

A television set

Electrons are controlled in a different way to create the picture in a TV set. At the rear of the set is an "electron gun." This shoots out a stream of free electrons which can travel in the tube because it has a vacuum – it has no air inside it. The electrons are directed toward the TV screen by two pairs of electrically-charged metal plates (the X and Y plates). The TV screen is painted with a special substance called a phosphor. When this is hit by the electron beam it emits light to create the TV picture.

Beam deflected up and down

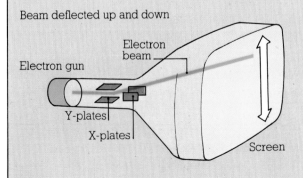

Electron gun

Electron beam

Y-plates

X-plates

Screen

Beam deflected from side to side

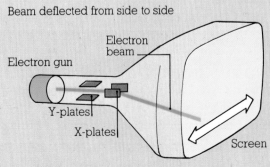

Electron gun

Electron beam

Y-plates

X-plates

Screen

Magnetism

A magnet exerts a strange force: it can defy gravity by picking up small pieces of iron such as pins and paperclips but has no effect at all on other metals – copper and silver coins, for instance, or aluminum. And if you place two toy magnets end to end in one way, they will "click" together. Placed the other way, they will force themselves apart. Furthermore, if you stroke an iron nail with a magnet, it seems to transfer some of its power, and the nail, too, becomes a magnet.

In fact, magnetic force is simply a relative of the electron-moving force that drives an electric current through a circuit. When a current travels through a wire, it is found that the wire has a magnetic field surrounding it. The greater the current, the stronger is this magnetic field. This property of electricity is used to create *electromagnets*, like the one shown here, operating in a scrapyard. A large electric current is sent through the dome hanging from the crane, activating the electromagnet, so that heavy iron girders can be picked up. The load can be dropped simply by switching off the current.

A toy magnet is a permanent magnet – it cannot be switched off. But its magnetism is also due to the movement of electrons – the electrons within each of the magnet's iron atoms. As these electrons circle the atomic nucleus, they create a weak magnetic field. In most kinds of atoms, the magnetic fields of the electrons cancel each other out. But iron atoms – and atoms of nickel and cobalt – can be made to arrange themselves in such a way that each small magnetic field reinforces the other, so that a complete block of iron can exert a strong magnetic force.

▷ Because magnets attract only iron, they can be used to sort iron from other metals, as well as for shifting heavy girders from place to place. Electromagnets are especially useful because they can be turned on and off. Smaller electromagnets are used in telephones, burglar alarms and motors.

An electromagnet

Inside an electromagnet there is a coil of wire with an iron core. When an electric current is passed through the coil, its magnetic field creates a magnetic field in the iron core – just as a toy magnet magnetizes an iron nail. When the current is switched off, the magnetism is lost – on our small version the paperclips will drop off.

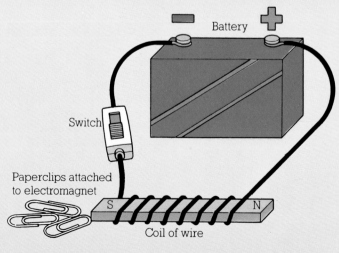

Battery

Switch

Paperclips attached to electromagnet

Coil of wire

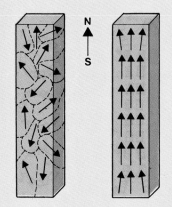

The domain theory
The atoms within an iron bar arrange themselves to create tiny "domains" of magnetism. These usually cancel each other out, but if the iron is placed in a magnetic field, these domains will line up in the same direction, so that the bar becomes a magnet itself.

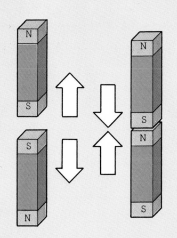

Attraction and repulsion
Magnetism in an iron bar is strongest at each end, or pole. These poles are called north and south. Similar poles repel each other, unlike poles attract.

Lines of Force

A magnetic field is the area in which magnetic force is exerted. Although it is invisible, we can show the pattern of this field by scattering small pieces of iron (iron filings) around a magnet placed on a sheet of paper. The iron filings become tiny magnets and line up with the magnetic field. For a bar magnet (1), the filings form curved loops from pole to pole. An electric coil (2), makes a similar pattern, and the lines of force run right through it. The magnetic field of a single electric wire (3), is very different, stretching out in circles round the wire.

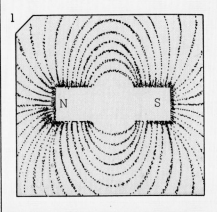

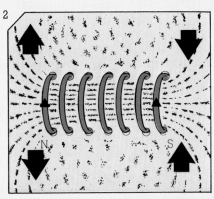

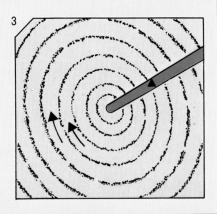

The Earth's Magnetic Field

When a magnet is suspended, one end points northward, while the other points to the south, so these ends are called the north and south poles respectively. The magnet lines itself up in this way because the Earth itself has a magnetic field. Following the rule of "unlike poles attract," the south pole of the Earth's magnetic field must lie in the north, to attract the north poles of other magnets. A compass needle is a small magnet that follows the lines of force of the Earth's magnetic field, to point to magnetic north. This is not the same as geographic north, but a map shows the difference.

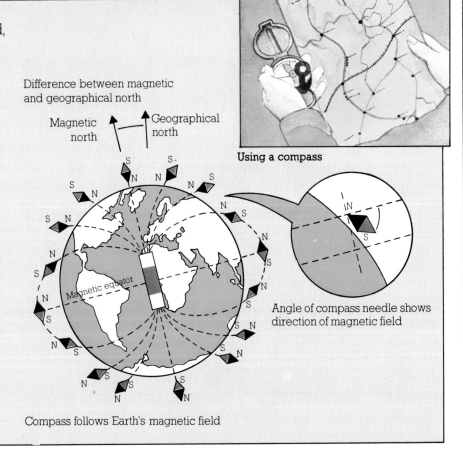

Using a compass

Difference between magnetic and geographical north

Magnetic north · Geographical north

Magnetic equator

Compass follows Earth's magnetic field

Angle of compass needle shows direction of magnetic field

Generators and Motors

A generator

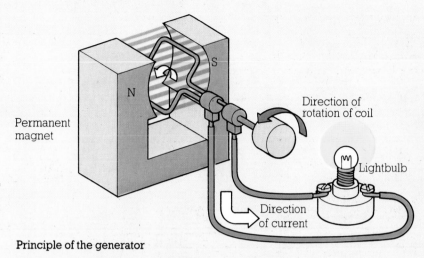
Principle of the generator

Permanent magnet

Direction of rotation of coil

Lightbulb

Direction of current

Generators

The close relationship between electricity and magnetism can be used to turn the energy of motion into electrical energy. This is what the generator on a bicycle does. Inside the generator there is a permanent magnet, with a loop of wire placed between its two poles. When the rear wheel turns, it turns this loop in the magnetic field. The magnetic force causes electrons in the wire to move, so creating electricity. The electricity flows in an electrical circuit to power the bicycle's lights. Larger generators produce our electricity in power stations.

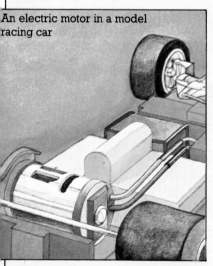
An electric motor in a model racing car

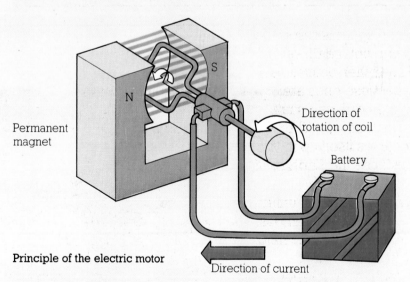
Principle of the electric motor

Permanent magnet

Direction of rotation of coil

Battery

Direction of current

Motors

An electric motor is the opposite of a generator. It uses a magnetic field to change electrical energy into the energy of motion. Again, a coil of wire is placed between the two poles of a permanent magnet. But in this case, we feed an electrical current into the coil. This current turns the coil into an electromagnet. The poles of the ordinary magnet repel the poles of the electromagnet, forcing the coil to spin round. In a model racing car, the coil is joined up to the driving shaft, so that the spinning coil turns the wheels and drives the car along. The electricity is supplied either by battery or other electric power source.

37

Glossary

Ampere The unit used to measure electric current. It indicates rate of flow of electrons in a conductor.

Amplitude The extent of a wave's vibration, measured as the height of the wave's peak or the depth of the wave's trough.

Atom The smallest individual unit of matter that can exist. Ninety-two kinds of atom occur naturally, each kind being a different element such as oxygen, carbon and iron.

Center of gravity The point at which the entire weight of a body may be thought of as being concentrated. If a body is supported at its center of gravity then it will remain in balance.

Centripetal force The force that is needed to keep an object moving in a circular path. It is directed towards the center of rotation, and changes the object's direction rather than its speed.

Electromagnetic spectrum This is the entire range of electromagnetic radiation of different wavelengths. It includes X rays, ultraviolet light, visible light, radiated heat and radio waves. This radiation is called electromagnetic because it consists of changes in electrical and magnetic fields traveling through space at the speed of light.

Electron A tiny particle that circles the nucleus of an atom, and carries the basic unit of negative electric charge. A flow of free electrons is an electric current.

Frequency The frequency of a wave is the number of complete waves occurring per second.

Friction This is the rubbing of one body against another. This can cause resistance to movement: it is easier to push a sheet of paper over a smooth table top than over a rough carpet, because the friction on the table top is less.

Gravity This is a force which causes free bodies to attract one another. The more massive a body is, the greater is the gravitational force it exerts.

Kinetic energy This is the scientific name for any energy that is connected with movement.

Magnetic field The area of space in which the forces caused by either a magnetic body, or a body that carries an electric current, can be detected.

Molecule A group of atoms held together by bonds to create a substance.

Proton A particle that goes to make up the heavy nucleus of an atom. It carries a positive electric charge equal, but opposite to that of the electron.

Ultraviolet light Part of the electromagnetic spectrum that has a wavelength slightly longer than that of violet light.

Volts The unit in which electron-moving force is measured.

Watts The unit which measures electrical power.

Wavelength The distance between the peak of one wave and the peak of the wave that follows it.

Index

PRINTED IN BELGIUM BY

INTERNATIONAL BOOK PRODUCTION